SHIPS and SAILORS

CONTENTS

Watts Books
London · New York · Sydney

KNOW YOUR SHIPS

THE SEA IS POWERFUL and often very dangerous. When the first ships set sail three thousand years ago, they stayed close to land. Since that time shipbuilders have continuously developed the design of hulls and rigging, sometimes with strange results. And sailors who chance their lives on the sea have always seen themselves as separate from landlubbers who live safely on shore.

Viking boats, built around AD 1000, were primarily rowing boats with a single woollen sail.

Galleasses were wider and deeper than galleys. They were used for carrying freight in the sixteenth and seventeenth centuries.

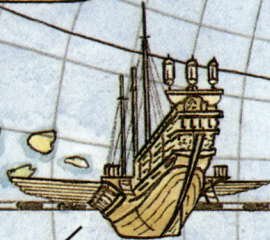

Arab dhows have been used for centuries for trading in the Indian Ocean.

A Mediterranean xebec favoured by eighteenth-century corsairs and pirates.

Caravels were used by Columbus alongside his carrack flagship in 1492.

A nineteenth-century passenger liner sailing with both steam and wind power.

A Russian circular warship, launched in 1875.

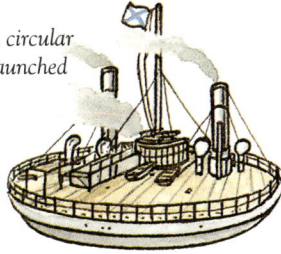

A clipper was a fast ship that 'clipped' the time of voyages during the nineteenth century.

Around 3000 years ago, the earliest Egyptian boats were rafts made of rushes.

A sixteenth-century deep sea galleon with rear guns for firing at pursuers.

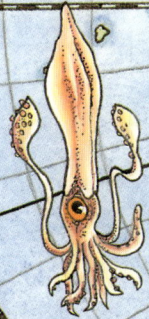

Carracks were broad, deep, fifteenth-century boats with high sterns and a high forecastle.

ANCIENT SHIPS

THE EARLIEST BOATS WERE MADE OF REEDS and sailed on the Nile. The largest were used to transport stones for the pyramids. A taut cable drawn from bow to stern kept the boat's shape. This could be slackened or tightened as the boat grew wet or dried out. It is possible that reed ships sailed out to sea.

THE EARLIEST PLANKED VESSELS also came from Egypt. They were developed from shallow barges with square ends. Shipbuilders shaped their prows so that they resembled the gracefully curved reed boats. When planks were added to the sides of a barge, it could be sailed out to sea. These were the earliest wooden ships.

THE PHOENICIANS were brilliant sailors. Around 600 BC the Pharaoh Necho asked them to find a new trade route by sailing from the Red Sea around Africa and back to Egypt. The Pharaoh thought it would be a simple task. In fact it took 2 years and about 26,000 km before they returned to Alexandria. And at the end of it all, no one is quite sure to this day whether they really did it.

The Phoenicians dominated trade across the Mediterranean from around 1000 BC. They built boats with broad, short hulls and large square sails to carry more cargo. These ships sailed as far as Cornwall, England, to trade for tin.

Early sails

On the Nile the wind often blows up the river, whilst the current flows down to the sea. Sails could be used to push a boat upstream and the current could be used to push it back downstream. The first sails were made from tall leaves.

Later, sails were made of reeds woven into a square attached to a mast. Early Egyptian ships with sails had a boom at the bottom of the sail which could be raised or lowered according to the wind.

Later still, lines were attached to the sail edges for trussing the sails before furling. These were known as brails. They make the rigging of a ship much simpler. Using the brails, sailors could expose the right area of sail for particular wind conditions. They could also alter the shape of the sail, making it triangular by pulling on certain brails.

Dug-outs were built from a single tree, and they could be quite big. Ancient British canoes have been found 10.6 metres long and nearly 1.5 metres wide. By attaching planks to ribs extending from a dug-out it could be made suitable for sea journeys. As planks were added the original dug-out log was reduced to a keel. Modern ships evolved from these boats.

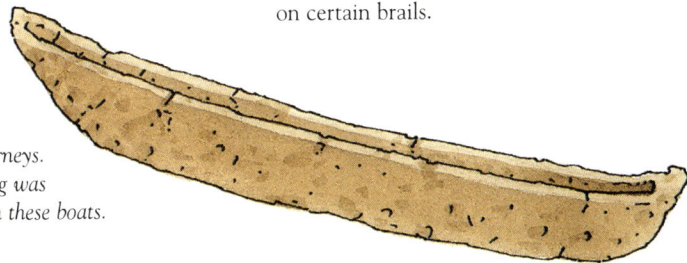

BY 3000 BC THE BABYLONIANS were using blown-up sheep skins to cross the river Euphrates. The air inside the skin was lighter than water.

GALLEYS AND SLAVES

A GALLEY is a long, slim ship powered by rowers. Athens in 480 BC had the most powerful navy in the Greek world. It possessed three main types of warship - biremes, triremes, and penteconters. The largest triremes were 37 metres long, and were rowed by 170 oarsmen. They were highly manoeuvrable and were used to ram and sink enemy ships. After ramming, a trireme could be rowed backwards at speed until free from its prey.

The lowest ranked officer maintained a watch on the bows.

The lowest port-holes on a trireme were only 45 centimetres above the waterline, and had to be sealed with leather to prevent water coming in when the ship was moving. As a punishment, men would be tied up with their heads sticking out of the port-holes.

The rams were placed below the waterline, so that a holed vessel was doomed to sink even in calm seas. They were sheathed in bronze.

THE ARSENAL IN VENICE was the dockyard at the centre of Venetian ship-building from AD 1200. It covered 24 hectares and produced many different vessels, from light war galleys to huge trading ships. An entire galley could be made in a week, thanks to a standardized production process. At its peak in the sixteenth century, 16,000 people were employed in foundries, armouries, and ropeworks.

THE EGYPTIAN PHARAOH, Ptolemy IV (reigned 221-204 BC), is said to have built a huge galley which was 122 metres long, 15 metres wide and needed 4,000 oarsmen to row it.

Triremes had up to five officers aboard. The chief was a wealthy political appointee, a member of the class who helped to pay for the ships.

The helmsman

IN 1571, a fleet of 273 Turkish galleys commanded by Ali Pasha, under the rule of Sultan Selim the Sot, engaged 200 European boats in the Battle of Lepanto. Although there were guns, sea warfare was still a matter of ramming and boarding. Only 47 Turkish vessels survived being captured, sunk or run aground. 12,000 Christian slaves were freed but 10,000 probably drowned with their ships.

Ancient states did not use slave oarsmen since able-bodied slaves were very expensive and would have to be kept even when there was no war. Oarsmen often rowed into battle in time to a piper playing a double-reeded instrument. Quite a speed could be built up as the steersman aimed the ship's ram at an enemy vessel.

OUTSIDE THE MEDITERRANEAN where slaves were less plentiful, the French used convicts and continued to build galleys until 1720. These galleys contained about 300 convicts, five to an oar. They were not allowed to move from their places, which were sections of board 45cm wide.

TO MAN THEIR GALLEYS, Muslims used Christian slaves and Christians used Muslims where possible. Slaves were chained by the ankle to their seats or their oars. Many never left their seats until they died.

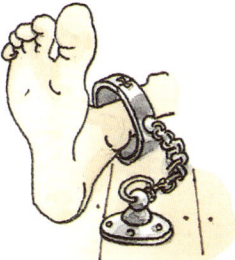

NORTHERN SEAS

FOR PROTECTION AGAINST PIRATES infesting the Baltic, the North Seas and the English Channel, merchants in Germany formed the Hanseatic League in 1241. By 1370 the League had its own fleets, armies, exchequer and government, and was made up of sixty-six cities and forty-four confederate cities. One group of Hanseatic merchants turned pirate and were known as the Victual Brothers. With the motto *Friends of God and Enemies of the World*, they plundered Hanseatic and English shipping. They were captured and executed in 1402.

IN THE THIRTEENTH CENTURY, the typical ship in northern waters was a square-rigged, single-masted sailing boat with no keel. During the next two centuries many features were introduced which transformed ships from coastal vessels to craft suitable for global exploration.

A bowsprit was added to take advantage of beam winds.

A deep-draughted hull meant more room for armaments and cargo.

Henry VII

HENRY VII OF ENGLAND developed the world's first ocean-going battle-fleet equipped with guns.

HENRY VIII'S SHIPWRIGHT, James Baker, moved the gun-mountings from the castles to gun ports at the sides of vessels, which increased stability. Some say he got this idea from a French shipwright called Descharges. The shift in shipbuilding from clinker-built hulls to caravels with flush-fitting planks happened at the same time as the cutting of gun ports.

VIKING LONGSHIPS were some 21 metres long, with keels shaped from a single piece of oak. Arising from the keel were the ribs to which the hull planks were lashed or nailed. The boats could reach speeds of up to ten knots.

OLAF, KING OF NORWAY in the tenth century, exemplified the Viking virtues. He was agile, strong and a great warrior. He could run along the oars above the water juggling three daggers while his men were rowing.

FOR CARGO VESSELS, Vikings used ships called knorrs, which were broader than longships, and sat deeper in the water.

BY TRADITION Viking chieftains were buried in special ships for their voyage to Valhalla, the feast-hall of dead heroes.

CHINESE SAILING SHIPS are called junks. In the Middle Ages they were in some ways technologically more advanced than ships in the West. In the fifteenth century, junks were the longest and safest ships in the world. They were capable of travelling great distances. Chinese merchants sailed to Indonesia, Ceylon, India, and as far as East Africa.

Chinese junks

Separate watertight compartments in the hull meant that if a hole was struck in one part of the ship, the water would not flow throughout and sink the vessel.

The high stern deck stayed quite dry in heavy seas and acted as a sail to turn the bows towards the wind when the ship was at anchor.

The sails were narrow panels tied to lines, rather than broad sheets attached directly to the mast. Much of the force of the wind was dispersed to the lines rather than against the mast which could snap during storms.

WOODEN WORLD

ALMOST ALL SHIPS WERE BUILT FROM WOOD until the nineteenth century. Many different types of wood were used: strong oak for the keel and hull, and tall, straight pines for the masts. A moderate-sized ship might take 2,000 hundred-year-old oak trees to build. The largest wooden sailing ship ever built was the *Great Republic*, 99 metres long and launched in 1853. Her mainmast was 40 metres high and 3.5 metres in diameter.

THE *GREAT MICHAEL* WAS LAUNCHED in Scotland in 1511. She was 73 metres long, 11 metres beam, and exhausted the timber of the county of Fifeshire during her construction. Timber had to be imported from mainland Europe to finish her.

THE *SOVEREIGN OF THE SEAS* WAS LAUNCHED in 1637 by Charles I and was so huge that six men could stand upright in her stern lantern. She cost £65,000 - over ten times the normal cost of a ship at this time.

THE FLOOR PLAN and side elevation of a ship were often drawn on to the walls and floor of a large building called a mould-loft. The ship's timbers were then cut to fit these same-size drawings.

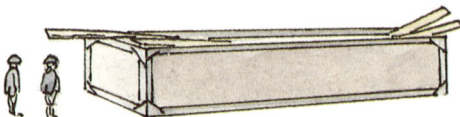

THE CURVED TIMBERS FOR THE HULL were traditionally pickled in huge vats to make the wood more pliable.

SLOOPS WERE SHIPS MUCH FAVOURED BY PIRATES, being light, fast and shallow-draughted. They were manoeuvrable in coastal waters and easy to beach or careen. Sloops tended to carry a mixture of light cannon and swivel guns. The large spar projecting over the bow almost doubled the sail area of the ship.

CAREENING involved laying the ship on its side to clear it of sea life - which would slow down the ship if allowed to build up. Careening was also done to remove the teredo worm, which ate at the ship's timbers, slowly eroding them. ▶

Since ancient times, ships have been lined with various metals such as lead. These were laid over fabric soaked with pitch or resin to resist the worm. At the end of the eighteenth century, ships were lined with copper sheathing fastened with copper nails.

CARAVELS developed from Portuguese fishing vessels, and brought in a new type of rigging - the fore-and-aft, lateen-rigged sail - which helped boats to sail much closer to the wind. ▶

THE EAST INDIAMAN, *Essex*, could set 63 sails in all - eight on the mainmast alone - from the mainsail to the stargazer. ▲

THE SHIPS in which Columbus sailed were of a new design. They had both traditional square sails and triangular ones, such as those used by Arab dhows. This rigging meant that the ships could maintain their course at a reasonable speed closer to the wind. ▶

A *pirate's guide to boarding*

Steer your ship to avoid the enemy's large cannon, while your marksmen aim to strike the enemy helmsman and the sailors manning the rigging. Manoeuvre under the stern of the ship and wedge the rudder.

Boarding should be attempted from several places at once, while gunners keep firing to keep the enemy beneath the hatches and away from their guns and cannon.

German boarders

In 1917, the British ships *Swift* and *Broke* engaged German destroyers off Zeebrugge. After ramming one of the destroyers, *Broke* was boarded by German sailors. In hand-to-hand fighting the British sailors used cutlasses to overcome the boarders. One German sailor was killed. ▼

LIFE ON BOARD

THE YOUNGEST SAILORS in the sixteenth and seventeenth centuries could go to sea as cabin-boys as young as ten years old or even younger. Others became sailors after being unable to find work on land. Some were forced to join by press gangs. It was not a popular career and it was very risky. At thirty, sailors were regarded as experienced old men - if they were still alive.

SAILORS HAD TO LIVE IN WHATEVER ROOM WAS LEFT after their ship was loaded with cargo and armaments. One hundred sailors might be crowded into a space fit for only 20. They slept on mats or hammocks strung up in the spaces between guns. Their tables were hung in the same narrow spaces.

SAILORS who survived shipwrecks or flogging were respected by their ship-mates.

INJURED SEAMEN would often suffer gangrene, and many died either from that or the primitive surgery they endured. The stumps of amputated limbs were sealed with hot tar or pitch.

TO GET RID OF THE RATS, lice, mites, beetles, cockroaches, and fleas that infested ships, seamen used gunpowder and fires to create smoke. However, Chinese pirates encouraged the rats aboard their junks because they ate them.

THE TOILETS on ships were called the heads and were placed in the bow or head of the ship.

THE SMELL OF URINE, vomit, rotting food, and dead rats made sailing ships stink so much that other ships could smell them over the horizon before they saw them.

rat

louse

biscuit beetle

German cockroach

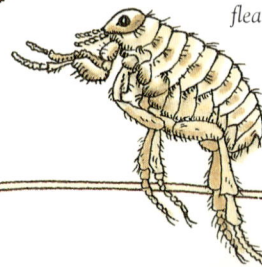

flea

SHIPS THAT SAILED ON LONG VOYAGES had to be self-sufficient in food and provisions. But in hot weather, after only a few days at sea, much of the food in the galley would crawl with flies and maggots.

IN THE EIGHTEENTH CENTURY the Royal Navy was short of men. To gain sailors it employed gangs to press or force men into service. To escape impressment sailors pretended to be paralysed or stupid. Some burnt themselves to make it look as if they had scurvy. ▶

A FAVOURITE PIRATE drink was a mixture of rum and gunpowder, and often a few other ingredients as well.

How to spot a sailor...

Rolling gait when walking

Baggy breeches of heavy rough nap, tarred against wetness

Blue and white linen shirt, blue or grey jacket

Seamen often used bits of hardened cheese or shark backbone as buttons

Grey stockings

Tattoos made by pricking skin and rubbing in ink or gunpowder

Tanned or reddened, wrinkled look

THE FIRST FIRE regulations on board a ship date from the fourteenth century. They tell ships' commanders to have two large casks aboard containing a few sheets of sail. Sailors should urinate into them, and the damp sheets could be used to smother any outbreak of fire.

EARLY SAILORS climbed the rigging naked in warm climates.

PUNISHMENT!

BECAUSE THE SEA CAN BE VERY DANGEROUS, it is important that ships' crews are efficient. Good sailors were skilled workmen, but they could be unruly. Captains were the absolute rulers of their ships and would discipline sailors harshly. Captains were often company men who shared in the profits at the end of a voyage. It was in their interest to make men work as hard and as cheaply as possible.

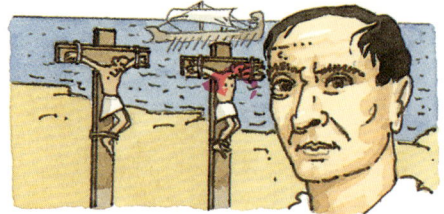

WHEN CAPTURED BY PIRATES, Julius Caesar was so offended by the low ransom demanded for his freedom, that he doubled it himself. When he was released he gathered a large force, returned to the pirates' lair and had his captors executed on the spot.

KEELHAULING was a very rare punishment. Men would either be lowered down one side of the boat and hauled under the keel to the other, or lowered beneath the bows and pulled by rope to the stern. The ancient Greeks practised keelhauling but as boats became larger it became impractical.

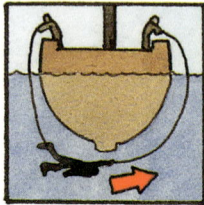

IT WAS ALSO THE GREEKS WHO introduced walking the plank. This was where prisoners' hands were tied and the prisoners were made to walk off the end of a plank attached to the side of a ship. This was, however, never widely practised.

IN ANCIENT TIMES the overseers of galley slaves commonly used a dried elephant's penis as a whip.

IMAGINE you are a seventeenth century sailor. Your captain has sentenced you to be punished, but you can choose which of these standard punishments you prefer...

Nightmare choice

being tied up and dropped over the stern of the ship to be towed behind

being flogged with the cat-o'-nine-tails

keelhauling

marooning

being beaten with beams of wood or iron bars

cleaning the heads

PRISONERS OF PIRATES might be forced into service. If not, they could be tortured by having their ears, noses, or other parts cut off.

A STANDARD PUNISHMENT for pirates in the seventeenth century was to tie them to a stake by the sea at low tide.

'SWEATING' WAS A PUNISHMENT in which a circle of candles was placed around the mast below decks and the prisoner forced to enter the circle. Then seamen would prod the prisoner with sharp implements, forcing him to run around the mast to the accompaniment of music until he dropped from heat exhaustion.

PIRATES COULD EXPECT LITTLE MERCY if they were caught. A common fate was to be hung from the yard-arm of their own ship.

WEIGHTS were attached to a prisoner's neck before he was dropped overboard to make sure he drowned swiftly.

ENGLAND, in the eighteenth century, sent convicts to Australia to serve their sentences rather than executing them. Discipline on board was very harsh, even women were flogged. Elizabeth Dudgeon spent nine days in irons for fighting, and a few days later was flogged for swearing at an officer.

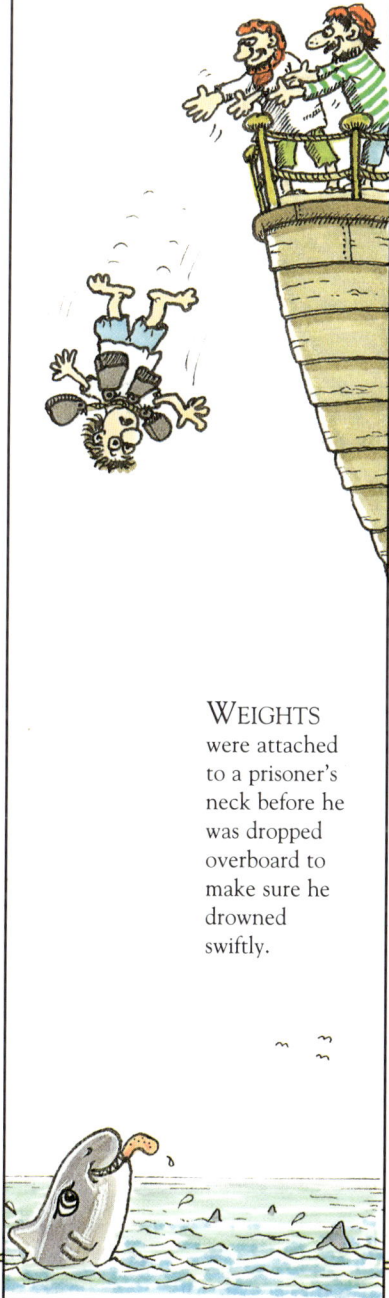

MERMAIDS *are the most famous 'sea females'. In 1771, a Dutch book described a sea creature called a 'sea wife' who was caught in the East Indies. She was about 1.5 metres long, with seaweed-coloured hair, olive skin, and webbed fingers. Around her waist was a belt of orange hair, bordered with blue. Her fins were green, and her face was grey. Pink hairs ran down her tail. She was kept in a vat of water for four days, uttering mouse-like cries before dying.* ➤

WOMEN WHO WENT TO SEA

WOMEN WHO SERIOUSLY WANTED TO BE SAILORS had, until recently, to disguise themselves as men. All other women on board were either prisoners, passengers, or the wives and girlfriends of sailors. The 'wives' of able seamen, however, were expected to carry gunpowder and tend to the wounded during a battle. Once in port, the ships quickly filled with women, who lived between decks with the sailors until the ship sailed. ▲

MARY BRYANT was a convict in Australia. In 1788 famine swept through New South Wales. Mary, with her husband William and their children, escaped in a single-masted boat to the island of Timor 5,236 km away, arriving three months later. They were then re-arrested and shipped to Java, where William and one son died. Mary was taken to London, another of her children dying on route. She ended up in Newgate Prison, and was finally pardoned in 1793.

CHING YIH SAOA was the widow of a Chinese pirate captain who took command of the pirate fleet in 1807 after her husband died. She enlarged the fleet to 1,800 junks crewed by 70,000 men and women. The women in Ching's fleet were as fierce as the men - one female captain used to fight with a sword in each hand, steering her junk at the same time. Madame Ching eventually accepted an amnesty from the Chinese government.

Seamen captured by Ching Yih's pirates were asked to join up. If they refused they would be strung up with their hands behind their backs until they either agreed or died in the ordeal.

Mary Read had been brought up in Britain as a boy by her mother. She served in the English army as a man before sailing to the West Indies in disguise. She served with Anne Bonny under the pirate captain, Calico Jack.

Anne Bonny wore trousers and a man's shirt; she became a pirate and fought with a cutlass and pistol. When she attempted to seduce another pirate she discovered 'him' to be another woman, Mary Read.

Mary
Read

Anne
Bonny

WOMEN PRISONERS could not expect to be treated gallantly. However, in one account of a privateer raid on a Spanish colonial town in Ecuador, the captain who led the raid wrote that his men had searched the women for gold chains by running their hands outside their dresses. They politely asked the women to remove the gold chains that they discovered.

IN 1899 CLARA BARTON, the founder of the American Red Cross, was the first woman to descend in a submarine off Sag Harbour in Long Island.

17

The Beaufort scale, numbered 0-17, measures the power of winds.

0: Calm	1: Light air	2: Light breeze	3: Gentle breeze	4: Moderate breeze	5: Fresh breeze

THE RAGING SEA

THE SEA WAS SPECIALLY DANGEROUS in earlier times when sailors were at the mercy of winds and currents, and without engines to help them.

IN A SUDDEN STORM sailors had to climb the rigging and furl all the sails whilst the ship tossed wildly in the waves. As they handled the ropes, their fingers were often stiff with cold. The top of a tall mast could sway through an arc of as much as 100 metres from one side to the other. A sailor at the top of the mast would accelerate through the air at a terrifying speed, as if on some nightmarish roller-coaster ride.

IN VERY ROUGH SEAS it is sometimes necessary for a ship to heave to, which means to stay as still as possible in the water. This is done using the motion of the waves past the rudder, or a small sail, to keep the ship in position. Otherwise she may end up sideways in the troughs, at the mercy of every wave.

6: Strong breeze 7: Moderate gale 8: Fresh gale 9: Strong gale 10: Whole gale 11: Storm 12-17: Hurricane

THE ROARING FORTIES is a belt of ocean below the equator where the winds always blow strongly from the west. Cape Horn on the southernmost tip of America juts into the Roaring Forties. It is the most dangerous sea passage in the world when rounded from east to west. Even when sailing before the wind from west to east the Roaring Forties are dangerous, because huge steep waves following behind may overwhelm the stern, or poop a vessel. Sailors on duty at the wheel are often forbidden to look behind them in case they become paralysed with fear at the sight of the huge waves.

THE CAPE OF GOOD HOPE produces unexpected freak waves and deep troughs. They are three or four times as large as normal waves and troughs. An additional danger is that the deep troughs, unlike extra-tall waves, are not visible until the ship is balanced on the edge of one. The ship plunges down two or three times the depth of the normal swell and sometimes isn't able to ride up the next wave, but plunges into the sea. During World War II, a cruiser plunged into a trough and the bridge, normally 18 metres above the waves, was covered in 0.6 metre of water.

THE ROUGH SEAS to the south of the Canary Islands are caused by a northerly swell hitting an off-shore wind. It prevented sailors exploring further south down the west coast of Africa until the fifteenth century. In 1434, a Portuguese captain called Gil Eanes braved the heavy seas. After 24 hours he broke through to calmer water, and opened southern Africa to Europeans.

A SEA ANCHOR IS A LARGE SAIL, attached to a line, which is thrown off the bow. The sail becomes waterlogged and acts as a drag to help a ship heave to. Nowadays the engineer can throw the ship's engine into reverse to counteract forward motion.

From 1898-1899 the Belgica was stuck in the Antarctic ice in the Bellingshausen Sea.

WRECKED!

THERE ARE MANY WAYS TO BE shipwrecked. Hidden rocks, floating icebergs, unseaworthy ships and treacherous wreckers - all can bring a ship to its doom. In the past, a main cause of disaster was sailing too close to a lee shore, where the wind blows the ship towards land.

SURVIVING A SHIPWRECK is only half the problem - after a ship has sunk, sailors have to live long enough to reach safety. To survive in cold water it's best to keep your clothes on, as water trapped inside them warms up and provides insulation.

IN 1865 THE ATHENS sank in heavy seas after being torn from her moorings and thrown on rocks. All 29 people on board died and only a pig was washed up alive.

THE SHIPWRECK OF VENTNOR in 1902 was unusual in that most of those on board were already dead before the ship struck a reef. It was carrying 499 dead Chinamen from New Zealand to be buried in China.

DR ALAIN BOMBARD, A FRENCHMAN, was shocked that men should die at sea when they were surrounded by water and had access to plentiful seafood. He was sure that given the right skills, wrecked sailors could survive for a very long time. To test his theory, he sailed from the Canary Islands to the West Indies in a 4.5 metres rubber open boat on 19 October 1953 - without any food or water. He drank 1½ pints of sea water every day, and ate fish he caught with a self-made harpoon. To combat scurvy he ate plankton scooped up with a cloth. He reached Barbados after 4,425 km and 65 days, having lost about 25 kilos, but otherwise quite well.

Wreckers

WRECKERS LIVED IN COASTAL COMMUNITIES. During stormy nights they would watch for the lights of stricken vessels, then plunder them and murder any survivors. It is said that wreckers would deliberately lure ships onto rocks by tying lights to horses tails, while beacons that warned ships away from hazardous rocks were deliberately not lit.

PETER SERRANO

lived on a rock in the middle of the Carribean for more than four years, living off shrimps, cockles, and turtles. He lived there naked after his clothes wore out. Eventually a passing ship took him home to Spain.

LIGHTHOUSES are normally used to warn ships away from dangerous coasts. However, the first lighthouse in England, built on Lizard Point, Cornwall in 1619, was said to have been built by Sir John Kelligrew to lure ships nearer to the shore where they fell prey to his pirate band.

THE EDDYSTONE LIGHTHOUSE AT PLYMOUTH was a wooden structure that burnt to the ground in 1755. In trying to put out the blaze, the 94 year old keeper swallowed some of the molten lead that streamed from the roof. When he died 12 days later, nearly a quarter of a kilo of lead was found in his stomach.

Life-jacket

Some ideas to help floating

In the late nineteenth century, a German invented a suitcase with panels on the top and a watertight seal, like the seal on a modern canoe. When shipwrecked the owner pulled out the panel, climbed in the suitcase and fitted the rubber seal around himself and floated away from the wreck.

French inventor, François Barathon, created the water-cycle lifeboat, made of a sail, two sets of cranks, and a bag on which the survivor sat. It was pedalled with both hands and feet to turn two propellers, one pointing downwards to keep the contraption upright, and one backwards to move it forwards.

STEAM AND IRON

WOODEN SHIPS are more expensive to build than iron ones, and steam power is faster and more reliable than wind power. It was inevitable that steam and iron would take over from wood and sail, although for a while passengers and shipowners were reluctant to change.

THE *DEMOLOGOS* was the first steam-driven warship. It was designed by Robert Fulton to break a British blockade of the USA.

AN OCEAN-GOING STEAMSHIP was built by Moses Rogers in Savannah, Georgia. She was rigged with sails as well as a coal-fired steam engine. Her paddles were designed to be lifted out of the water when they were not in use and her main method of propulsion was still wind. Passengers were afraid to sail in her. So in 1819 Rogers, himself, sailed her to Russia and back with no problems. Unfortunately for Rogers, people still would not travel in her under steam and the ship spent the rest of her days as a sailing vessel.

Screws v. paddles

SCREWS ARE EFFICIENT IN HIGH THRUST, LOW SPEED situations, but have struts and shafts that increase water resistance. The British Admiralty staged a 'tug of war' in 1845 between two 800 tonne vessels of equal horsepower, the paddle-driven *Alecto* and the screw-driven *Rattler*. The *Rattler* won by towing the *Alecto* away at about 2½ knots.

Early steamships were mostly driven by paddles, which are very efficient in the right conditions. However, when the seas are heavy, paddles tend to come out of the water as the ship rolls. With heavy loads, high thrust and low speeds, as occurs for example with tugs towing heavy vessels, the paddle slips in the water.

Ironsides

IRONCLAD WARSHIPS were built in Korea in the sixteenth century. They were low-decked junks covered with an iron dome and surrounded by iron spikes to prevent boarding. They had iron rams and cannon could be fired through ports in the armour plating. They were known as tortoise boats and were used to defeat the Japanese at the end of the century.

THE *GREAT WESTERN*, built by Isambard Kingdom Brunel, proved that larger ships need proportionally less fuel than smaller ships. The reason is that the surface area of the hull in the water determines the power needed to move the ship, not the space inside the hull. The larger the ship the smaller its surface in proportion to the space inside it. A rival company launched the *Sirius*, a smaller craft, ahead of the *Great Western*. The *Great Western*, nearly twice the size of the *Sirius* and sailing from harbour four days after her, arrived at New York only a few hours behind.

The first battle between two iron-clad ships took place in March 1862 during the American Civil War, when the Monitor from the South fought the Merrimac from the North. It was a draw.

THE *GREAT BRITAIN* WAS DESIGNED by Brunel. As with the planks of a clinker-built boat, the iron plates of the *Great Britain* overlapped. Brunel kept enlarging the ship throughout the design stages, earning it the nickname *Mammoth*. Eventually, these endless changes led to the death of his engine designer when, having laboured over the massive engines for a paddle steamer, he saw them scrapped.

Very long ships must be able to bend or flex with the sea, so that they don't break apart under the enormous forces acting on their great length.

A large fully-laden oil tanker will take up to 32 km to stop.

GIANT SHIPS

THE LARGEST EARLY SHIPS were cargo ships. Then came the giant nineteenth century passenger liners. Today the largest ships afloat are again cargo ships - the giant oil tankers. The oil tanker *Seawise Giant* is nearly half a kilometre long with a draught of 24.3 metres.

AN OIL TANKER is a skin of metal separating one liquid - oil, from another liquid - sea water. If it is not controlled, the oil will slosh from side to side within the tanker, causing it to roll violently and sink. Oil tankers are divided into many small compartments to restrict the movement of the oil.

GIANT SHIPS consume an enormous amount of fuel. The *Oceanic*, a luxury passenger liner launched in 1899, was 214.5 metres long and consumed 400 tonnes of coal a day. Her lavatories were the most luxurious afloat at the time, being made of white marble.

ISAMBARD KINGDOM BRUNEL DESIGNED THE *GREAT EASTERN* to be large enough to steam from Britain to Australia without refuelling. When launched, the *Great Eastern* was five times larger than the largest steamship then afloat, and could carry 4,000 passengers. She was propelled by two 17.6 metre high paddles, an 8.5 metre high screw, and 6,000 metres of sail. It took a month to launch the *Great Eastern*, moving her 10 metres to the water.

The larger the ship, the more comfortable it is to ride. The development of geared turbines enabled huge ships to be driven more efficiently at high power.

On large tankers sailors use motorbikes to move about the deck in calm weather!

THE *THOMAS W. LAWSON* was a steel-hulled schooner built in 1902. She had 7 masts 59.4 metres high. The sails were controlled by a clever system of steam winches and the whole ship only required 16 sailors.

THE NUCLEAR-POWERED AIRCRAFT CARRIER *NIMITZ* was launched in 1972. Her overall length is 332.9 metres and she can carry about 90 aircraft serviced by 6,300 sailors and air crew. She can cruise at 30 knots for about 1.6 million kilometres without refuelling.

UNTIL 1940 THE HEAVIEST BATTLESHIP AFLOAT WAS THE *BISMARCK*, pride of the German navy. She displaced around 50,000 tonnes of water and carried eight 38 cm guns and twelve 15.2 cm guns. It took the combined actions of nineteen British warships five days to sink her.

THE 45.7 CM GUNS installed on the World War II Japanese battleships *Yamato* and *Musashi* had a range of 43 km and fired shells weighing 1, 450 kg.

SUBMARINES

'AND ALSO IT IS POSSIBLE to make a ship or boat that may goe under the water unto the bottome, and so come up againe at your pleasure....' (William Bourne, *Inventions and Devises*, 1578). This is the first description of a self-propelled submarine, although submarines have been a challenge to ship designers since at least the time of Alexander the Great (356–323 BC).

Alexander is said to have gone underwater in a primitive diving bell.

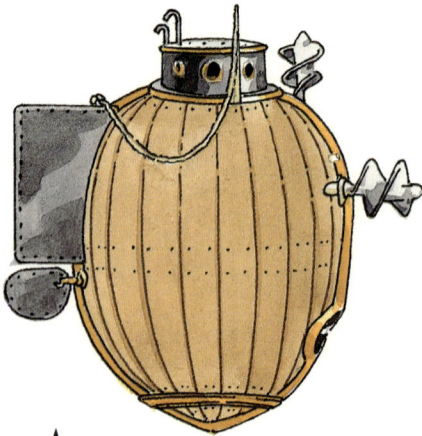

IN 1776, during the American War of Independence, the American inventor David Bushnell developed a one-man submarine called *The Turtle*. Powered by a hand-cranked propeller, it carried a bomb. This was to be screwed onto the wooden hull of the *Eagle*, a British ship blockading the Hudson River. Unfortunately, the *Eagle*'s copper sheathing made the attachment impossible. The bomb was jettisoned and went off harmlessly.

WILLIAM BOURNE first described the principle of the submersible boat, but it was not until 1620 that a true submarine was constructed by Cornelius van Drebel. He demonstrated his device in the River Thames, King James I being one of the observers. Though successfully completing its journey the crew were in bad shape afterwards, as there was no way to replace the oxygen which they had used up. Van Drebel went on to produce a more efficient twelve-oared underwater boat in 1624.

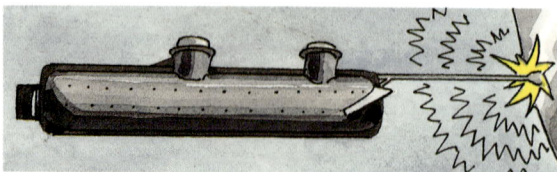

IN 1864, DURING THE AMERICAN CIVIL WAR, an Alabama regiment launched the submarine *H L Hunley*, powered by eight men cranking a propeller. The *Hunley*'s spar-mounted torpedo blew a hole in the union ship *Housatonic*, but the explosion also destroyed the *Hunley*. The *Hunley*'s remains were discovered in 1995.

IN 1800, ROBERT FULTON demonstrated his sail-powered *Nautilus* to the French Navy for use against the British. Although Fulton successfully destroyed an old schooner in Brest harbour, Napoleon did not take up the idea. He then approached the British Navy, but they also turned down his invention. Fulton died in 1815 before he could complete the *Mute*, a steam-powered submarine.

DURING WORLD WAR I, the British attempted to use sea lions to locate submarine propeller noise. However, they were unable to distinguish between surface and submarine vessels.

Detecting submarines ▶

ONCE DETECTED, submarines risk being bombed by depth charges. Since their engines can be heard by sonar, and they are sitting targets if they stay still, most commanders would try to sneak their submarines away at the lowest engine power.

SONAR DETECTS SOUND WAVES emitted by a submarine. But about 61 metres below the surface there is a sudden change in water temperature which reflects the sound waves. A submarine diving below this layer can remain hidden. Submarines in World War II would retreat beneath the thermal layer to avoid detection.

IN 1915, THE BRITISH ADMIRALTY decided to build a combination of destroyer and submarine. The K-boats were about 100 metres long and heavier than the longest destroyer. They were very difficult to pilot and could only dive after five minutes preparation, whereas the enemy U-boats could dive in 90 seconds. K-3 sank on a test dive, nearly drowning the future King George VI. Despite never seeing enemy action the K-boats caused the death of 270 of their own crews.

DURING WORLD WAR II, THE JAPANESE built several huge underwater aircraft carriers. They were 123 metres long, with a hangar of 3.6 metres by 31 metres, which could contain three float-planes and a dismantled fourth. ▶

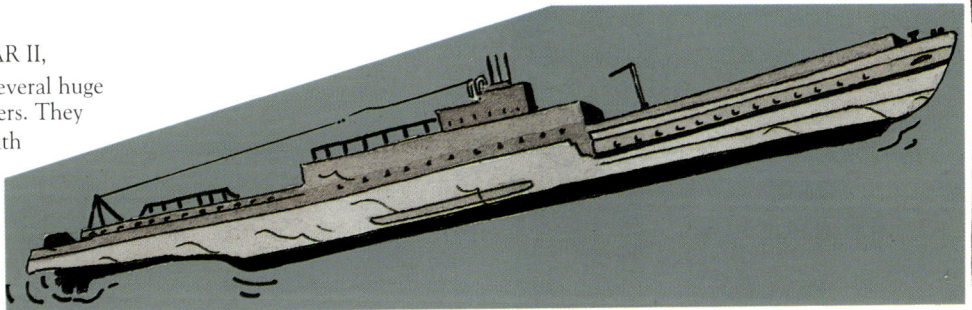

Modern nuclear submarines can spend up to three months at a time under water.

THE US built the first nuclear-powered submarine, USS Nautilus, which was launched in 1955. She was 98.7 metres long, 26.8 metres wide and carried 105 crew at a speed of 20 knots underwater. She was the first submarine to sail under the polar ice pack.

STRANGE SHIPS

SHIPS OFTEN SEEM TO LOOK VERY MUCH ALIKE.
But some ships have been strikingly different. They
have had special jobs to do, or have been designed to
do common jobs more efficiently.

WHEN CHRISTOPHER COCKERELL
was developing the hovercraft in 1950 he
built a prototype with his wife's vacuum
cleaner and an old boat.

A SHIP WAS SPECIALLY CONSTRUCTED TO CARRY
CLEOPATRA'S NEEDLE, a 20 metre, 203 tonne ancient
Egyptian obelisk, from Alexandria to London. John and
Waynman Dixon designed and built the *Cleopatra*. The ship was
an iron cylinder 28.3 metres long, 4.5 metres wide with 10 watertight compartments. The *Cleopatra* left Alexandria in September
1877 and arrived in London during January 1878. It was delayed
due to bad weather.

Prototype hovercraft

A slot was cut in the bow of a punt.

*The punt was turned upside down and a vacuum cleaner
with air-flow reversed was attached so that the air was
blowing through the slot and underneath the punt.*

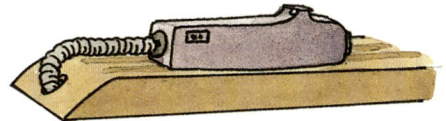

*When paddling the punt forwards, on water, the
resistance of the water was reduced by the flow of air.*

ANTON FLETTNER harnessed wind pressure
to drive a ship that used rotors 19.8 metres high
and 3 metres in diameter. Wind pressure in a
revolving disk is much greater than in a normal
sail. But the ship, despite being cheap to run,
suffered mechanical failure due to the vibration
caused by the rotor.

IN THE NINETEENTH CENTURY SIR HENRY BESSEMER
invented a 'swinging' saloon to stay level when ships sailed through
heavy seas. But it made the motion worse for those inside the saloon
than those on the deck! Also the ship suffered steering problems and
crashed into the piers at Calais and Dover.

ON D-DAY, blockships with specially modified superstructures were sailed across the English Channel. They were sunk so that their decks could serve as harbours for landing vehicles, soldiers, and supplies to attack the German fortifications. About a third of a million men were landed, with 54,000 vehicles and 100,000 tonnes of stores.

TO SUPPLY FUEL FOR THE INVASION FORCE, specially modified tugs crossed the channel, laying continuous lengths of flexible piping along the seabed. Eleven pipelines supplying 3,150 tonnes of fuel were in place by April 1945.

ON D-DAY, 6 JUNE 1944, OVER 1,000 ships crossed the English Channel to invade German-occupied France. To help unload weapons and vehicles, 11 km of piers and jetties were towed over the channel.

Ice-ships

AIR PATROLS GUARDED CONVOYS OF SHIPS against attack by U-boats in World War II. As an alternative to huge and expensive aircraft carriers, a British inventor thought of man-made icebergs. These would be rectangular in shape, 91 metres wide and 305 metres long, with flat tops and hollowed centres for hangars and living quarters. It was discovered that the addition of 10% wood pulp made ice as strong as concrete yet easy to work. Unfortunately, the ice-ships cost at least as much to build as conventional aircraft carriers and the project was never completed.

THE CONNECTOR was built in three hinged sections. This supposedly enabled it to ride smoothly through rough seas, as well as be disconnected for easy loading and unloading. She was built around 1850.

NAVIGATION

IT'S ALL VERY WELL TO BUILD A SHIP, but not much use if you don't know where you're going. Water looks much the same all over the world. It's difficult to work out where you are in the middle of an ocean. Early sailors stuck close to shore and navigated by landmarks. Further out to sea they made use of the Sun, stars, winds and currents. Clouds and birds were a sign that land was close.

SOME CREATURES have an inborn sense of direction. It is thought to be related to sensitivity to the Earth's magnetic field. In humans it is much less well developed than in animals such as homing pigeons, which can navigate their way across thousands of miles. So human sailors need help.

EARLY MEDITERRANEAN SAILORS divided the wind into eight directions, known as the Wind Rose. The Wind Rose gave rise to the first written guide to navigation, the Periplus. Routes from port to port were described in terms of wind direction. Andronicus of Cyrrhus built an eight-sided Tower of the Winds around 100 BC, to measure wind direction.

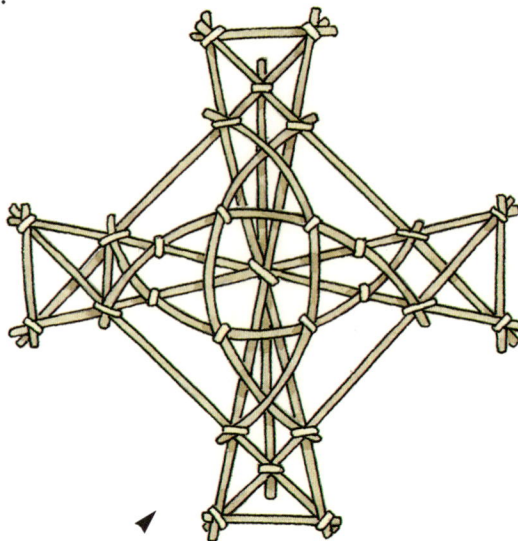

THE POLYNESIANS could tell where they were in the Pacific by the rocking of the waves and the colour of the water. The Mattang is a device made of bamboo sticks, used to teach young Polynesians about how waves move.

Some logs were carved to represent sea-birds or fish.

IN 1637 RICHARD NORWOOD described the use of a 28 second hour-glass and a rope with knots tied in it at 120 cm intervals. The rope was attached to a triangular piece of wood, which was dropped over the stern. As the ship moved away, the rope unrolled. If the sand in the hour-glass ran out before the first knot appeared, the ship was travelling at one knot or 1.15mph. This apparatus became known as a log.

In 1688 Humphry Cole invented the patent log - a vaned rotor which was towed behind a ship. As the ship moved, the vanes turned and the revolutions were counted to give the speed of the ship.

Longitude and latitude

Longitude is the measurement of position east/west. Latitude is the measurement of position north/south. In the second century BC, Hipparchus, an ancient Greek, proposed the system of latitude and longitude we use today. Latitude can be calculated by measuring the length of a shadow cast by a stick at a particular time of day. Pytheas used this method for his epic voyage to the Arctic circle.

THE VIKINGS COULD CALCULATE THEIR LATITUDE but not their longitude, which could not be calculated until the eighteenth century when there were accurate clocks. One way to cross the Atlantic from Europe to their colonies in Greenland was to sail due north until they reached the latitude of their destination and then turn left.

OCEAN DEPTHS are measured in fathoms of 1.8 metres. These were originally measured with weighted lines thrown overboard. The weights also held tallow fat which picked up samples from the seabed, to see if the samples agreed with information given on maps. ➤

Instruments for measuring latitude

ASTROLABE: first used around the third century BC, for observing the position of heavenly bodies. In the Middle Ages it became a navigational instrument.

CROSS STAFF: a three foot length of wood fitted with a sliding crosspiece. The crosspiece is pushed along the staff until its lower end is level with the horizon and its upper end with the Pole Star. The altitude of the Pole Star can then be read and the latitude calculated.

SEXTANT: is used to measure the angle between the horizon and the Sun or a star. This angle can be used to determine the latitude.

QUADRANT: invented independently of each other by Thomas Godfrey in 1730 and by John Hadley in 1731.

RADAR SYSTEMS bounce radio waves off objects to plot their position. Radar was one of the best kept secrets of World War II. Germany and Japan could not understand how their ships were so easily detected. ➤

INDEX

First published in 1996 by
Watts Books
96 Leonard Street
London
EC2A 4RH

Franklin Watts Australia
14 Mars Road
Lane Cove
NSW 2060

UK ISBN: 0 7496 2000 5
10 9 8 7 6 5 4 3 2 1
A CIP catalogue record for this book is
available from the British Library
Dewey Decimal Classification: 387.5

© 1996 Lazy Summer Books Ltd
Illustrated by Lazy Summer Books Ltd
   and Denise Heywood

Printed in Belgium

PRINTED IN BELGIUM BY
proost
INTERNATIONAL BOOK PRODUCTION